THE SECRETS
OF A #1 SALESMAN

BY
SOLOMON
HICKS
WITH MICHELLE JONES

HICKS GLOBAL
ENTERPRISES

First Edition

Printed in Indonesia

Cover Design by 3rd Generation Graphix of Atlanta, GA
Interiors by Page Design of Los Angeles, CA

ISBN-13: 978-0-9789346-1-3
ISBN-10: 0-9789346-1-X

DEDICATION

To every man and woman who sells.
There is room at the top for you.

TABLE OF
CONTENTS

21 SECRETS OF A #1 SALESMAN

KEEP THE LIGHT ON INSIDE YOU   35

21 SECRETS OF A #1 SALESMAN

USE THE LIGHT ON AROUND YOU   65

21 SECRETS OF A #1 SALESMAN

LEAVE THE LIGHT ON BEHIND YOU 95

31 DAYS OF WISDOM

Before you begin…

Promise yourself...

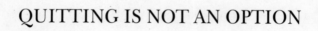
QUITTING IS NOT AN OPTION

CHAPTER ZERO

BRING MORE TO THE TABLE THAN YOUR APPETITE

❧❧

This book begins *before* the first chapter. That's because you began before you made your first sale. You are bigger than your numbers, better than the most enthusiastic "yes" and stronger than the loudest "no."

Before we were salespeople, we were *people*. Sales don't make the man. The man (or the woman) makes the sales.

I want to begin here because I don't want this to be just another book about managing your behavior. I have no desire to tell you to do this thing or that so you can become a pleasing replica of my success, my opinions, and my dreams.

That's how you treat little children and people you don't know or care about. You are obviously not a child, so there is no need to give that thought any more consideration. I would, however, like to spend a little time addressing the other two, because you may be thinking, "True, I'm not a child, but I could be counted among those he doesn't know or care about."

Not true. I do know you, and I do care about you.

If your business is sales, I know you. If you have known the highs of hitting your numbers or the low feelings of insecurity and loneliness that come with missing the mark, I know you. Have you ever been disappointed, afraid, or questioned your sanity for placing your future in the hands of people who may or may not want what you have to offer? Do you find yourself wondering if you can live up to all those positive affirmations you post on your laptop or carry in your wallet? Then I know you. I know you because I *am* you. Your journey is my journey.

We are connected by our experiences. We share many of the same desires. Our yardsticks for measuring success and failure aren't too different from one another. I know you. We know each other.

How then can I care about my own success and not care about yours? We are in this business together. We rise and fall together. If that sounds a bit dramatic, then I have said it well.

In sales, more than any other vocation, the best of us are inspired by and taught by the success of others. Tools in the hand of one top performer become tools for all of us if he's willing to share, and sometimes if he isn't.

If we are good, we will mold proven techniques to our particular shape, and if we're honest, we can admit our indebtedness to others for much of what we do well. Whether it's for the jokes we tell to break the ice or our most effective closing questions, we depend on one another.

I am a resource junkie. From the day I started my first sales job to this one—40 years at this writing—I have devoured hundreds of books, tapes, and CD's on selling. If there is a good talk, workshop, or seminar nearby, I am there when the doors open and until they close. I am a learner at heart, not ashamed to admit what I don't know, but unwilling to be ignorant for long.

In all my reading and hearing, though, I have seldom come across an author, speaker, coach or teacher who has accomplished what I have. Some of the best techniques have come to me from men and women who have far fewer years in this business than I, and only a fraction of the awards and recognition. That tells me something significant: We are always bigger than what we learn, and every teacher is a servant to his or her students.

Most of us get this idea turned around. We worship our teachers and hope to be like them one day. We see knowledge and understanding as a vast pool that will drown us if we go too deeply into it.

The truth is the student gives his teacher purpose and significance. How much value is there in a teacher if no one is learning? What good is knowledge unknown or understanding misunderstood? All of the experience and instruction we receive should become a part of us. We were never meant to be swallowed up by it.

This is the mind I want you to bring to this book. Be served by what you find in it, because that is my intention. Affirm and confirm *my* calling by taking what I have to offer and making something better out of it.

This book is my small contribution to your significance. Calling it small is not my attempt at humility. I believe it will add much value to whatever you're doing or I would not have written it. "Small" is what I hope it will be placed next to what you will one day contribute to others.

With that in mind, I offer you one bit of advice as you read: Bring more to the table than your appetite. Come with more than an expectation to get a few tips on what to say to a prospect or how to manage your time. By all means, please don't come on the other extreme, as if you are an ignorant sojourner in search of an oracle. I am not your savior. You don't need one here.

Rather than just expecting, come *expressing*. As you learn what's in these pages, commit yourself to adding each captured truth to your expression of yourself. You are what matters. Allow whatever wisdom you find here to uncover your brilliance so that you can shine for others.

Remember tomorrow.

That seems like an oxymoron, doesn't it? Remembering is for yesterday, for things already in the past, right? That is true with one exception.

Where do your dreams live?

Have you had "glimpses" of who you really are? Is there a deep ache in your insides to be loosed of everything that is not "like" you? Come to this book confident that your destiny precedes you and that whatever I have to offer you will help light the way to it. Come knowing that there is something greater than you and me.

I called this book "The Secret Life of a #1 Salesman" because 40 years in sales has taught me that success is lived from the inside out. It is a process of discovering and uncovering my inner man, strengthening myself where I'm weak, pouring out what I have, and believing always that no matter what my circumstances tell me, I will prevail.

You are a magnificent secret waiting to be told to the world. Selling becomes a vehicle to let others in on the secret. Selling is how you are "shared" with others.

Selling is not my gift. It used to bother me to think of myself that way. Long before I had my first number one trophy, I would look at "true salesmen," the glib, quick-on-their-feet superstars in the business, and wish I was more like them. I would stand in the mirror for countless hours imitating them. I asked my wife to watch me "perform" my sales pitch and offer her critique.

I learned to play the part of a top seller well enough to post acceptable numbers, but there was always something inauthentic about it. Somewhere there was a voice inside me saying, "You are pretending because you're afraid you're not good enough on your own. You are a fraud. One day you will be found out."

Then I discovered that my joy in this business came not from selling, but from listening, caring, serving, and sharing what I was learning with others. Selling was a way to experience those things. From then on, my life and work were transformed. I still wanted to be number one, but now it didn't just mean I had better numbers than everyone else. It meant that people knew they were being heard. It meant lives were changed and I had something to do with that.

I love what I do because I love *doing* it. I'm inspired by it, and excited by it. I'm good at what I do, and I don't have to pretend to be someone else while I do it. I'm successful at it because I am who I was made to be.

If you are Michael Jordan, you love basketball, and you want to be as good as the guys who came before you, the Wilt Chamberlains and the Kareem Abdul-Jabbars. You've seen them play. They're exceptional, but something deep inside is whispering, "You are not them."

THE SECRET LIFE OF A #1 SALESMAN

Somewhere inside, you are longing to be *Air*. So you learn every play, and play every game to the best of your ability. Then something clicks into place and *Air* Jordan suits up for a game. Michael runs, but Air flies. Michael jumps. Air soars.

Once Air Jordan is free, Michael is free. He does what he does as only he can. He succeeds as only he can. Then one day he is seen by players like Allen Iverson, LaBron James, and Yao Ming, and they are inspired, by his example, to put their unique imprint on the sky and beyond.

I want you free to be everything you can imagine and more. I'm familiar with the view from the top, and guess what. There is room up here for you. I don't have to get out of the way for you to have it. It's waiting for you…if you just don't quit.

Wherever you are, don't give up. Don't turn back.

I can't see the person reading these pages, but I know that selling is not always fun. We are not always happy, even when we are smiling.

Much of what we do is "heart work." It is the establishing and maintaining of relationships. It is walking with people, sometimes through some very difficult seasons. We have to be strong for them, even when we're weak. We offer hope, while we ourselves are discouraged.

If you are in sales, you have already learned to hide your real feelings behind a veil of competence. Let's leave our masks at the door as we walk through these pages, okay? Remember, we know each other.

Somebody picked up this book and you're not thinking about being number one. You'd be happy to crack the top 200. You can't even imagine past that. Somebody's weary. Maybe you're discouraged, or desperate to see just a little light after a string of bad weeks.

When I think about writing a book that I hope will inspire and motivate, I have two choices. I can pump you up with the highlights of my career and send you away feeling good…for a little while.

Or I can tell you the <u>whole</u> truth. That being number one means sacrifice and effort. That I didn't just jump from peak to peak. There were deep valleys in between.

I choose the truth. I choose it because I want you to have hope. I want you to know that everything you desire is within your reach, because you and I are not so different. We've all had setbacks. We've all heard "no" more times than we care to.

We have all had challenges. We have all been shaped by the events and experiences of our lives. We all bring our emotional scars and bruises with us to the office, and out on every sales call.

We all have to overcome. I'm living proof that you <u>can</u> overcome if you don't quit. I know that nothing is impossible for the man or woman who believes.

I grew up poor and in the segregated South. There were restaurants where I could work as a cook or a bus boy, but I could not walk through the front door, or sit down at the counter to eat at them. As a teenager, I cleaned water fountains that I could not legally drink from.

I am a college drop out because a segregated public school system let its teachers use old, outdated *elementary* school books to educate us in high school. They weren't really trying to prepare us for higher education. Many of us were told that we'd be lucky if we grew up and became farmers, but not to expect much beyond that.

On my first sales job, I made no salary, and I was cheated out of all my commissions.

Prudential Financial gave me my second sales job. I was fired during my first week, when they found out I didn't have a car or a home phone. I begged my manager to reconsider. I told him he wouldn't be sorry. He wasn't. I made Rookie of the Year, and today, I am the most successful agent in that company's history.

I want to meet you wherever you are. If you're already up, I know how to go higher. If you're down, I am familiar with that place too. My point is this: There is no place you cannot succeed from. When you've read the last page of this book, if you believe that, I will be satisfied.

I will meet you in chapter one and we'll walk together. My hope is that along the way, you will receive some tools and make them your own. My desire is that you would be encouraged and inspired, that your inner person would be strengthened and restored. I want you to uncover your greatness and unleash your power. My dream is simply this: that you would know the wonderful truth about yourself, and that it would make you free.

CHAPTER ONE

LIGHTEN UP

❧❧

Three simple rules govern every waking moment of my life. They define and shape me. I am directed by the path they have revealed to me. They are foundational to my success because every routine or discipline I create for myself finds its origin in them. Plainly communicated, they are:

KEEP THE LIGHT ON INSIDE YOU
USE THE LIGHT ON AROUND YOU
LEAVE THE LIGHT ON BEHIND YOU

Your "light" is simply the Truth of your unique significance. Your light says you matter in and to the world, there is a plan and a path for you, and that you were designed to succeed. Yes, I said you were *DESIGNED* to succeed.

There is order in all of nature. We were not created haphazardly. I happen to believe that an all-knowing, ever-present, sovereign God made us all with a purpose and an idea in mind. I would stake my life on it. I have in fact.

You may believe that. You may not. It doesn't matter. Even science tells us that every living thing is alive because it has found a way to succeed in this world. They say there is undeniable order working in nature and that if something is not fit to survive, it dies.

Whatever you believe, you cannot escape the fact that if something is living, it should be succeeding. The fact that we are human means we have a choice about *how* we succeed.

You and I have chosen to succeed at selling.

Before we move on, let me applaud your courage. Telling people you're a salesman is not always met with lots of enthusiasm. You see it's hard for people to continue a conversation with us once they find out what we do. They think if they continue talking and say something like, "Really? What do you sell?" they're opening themselves up for our "spiel" and before they know it, we've skipped town with their kids' college fund.

As a rule, people think they can't trust us. I believe Hollywood and the media have done a lot to contribute to the negative image of salesmen. They paint us as hucksters out to make a dollar, slick, smooth talkers hawking unreliable wares to unsuspecting sheep. We talk fast and lie faster. We shake your hand and shake you down at the same time.

I'm sure those stereotypes are true of some. But those kinds of people don't last long in a profession built on credibility and reputation. I also think that people aren't as dull as some think they are. 70% of communication is non-verbal. The average shyster usually reveals himself quickly to a person of even average intelligence.

I believe what we do is noble and I think those who are the best at it and who last the longest are some of the most decent people I know. Most of us believe that what we sell adds value to the lives of others. I sell life insurance and financial products and services. I have seen too many lives impacted by what I do to believe otherwise.

One psychological study found that the average person is thinking about him- or herself 94% of the time. If the average salesman thought about himself that much—in other words, if he paid only 6% of his attention to the needs of others—he wouldn't be in this business for very long.

Four decades in sales has taken me all over the world. I have met, mentored, and become friends with sales professionals from Asia, Europe, Africa, and even "down under" in Australia and New Zealand. There are language and cultural differences, and some variations in business practices. Consistent across continents is a generosity of spirit that runs through every sales community I have had the privilege of connecting with.

Good salespeople are always giving. We teach even when we're not selling. We pay attention. I like to think we're better husbands and wives than most (when we're home) because of what we do. We are natural encouragers because so often we have to encourage ourselves.

Certainly we're not perfect. We are competitive, egotistical at times, and driven. Sometimes our kids would like to see more of us. (Hopefully they know that we would like to see more of them too.) We have very high "highs" and very low "lows," and it's not always easy to tell which is which.

Still, with all our faults—our very *human* faults—I am proud of who we are and what we do. We are businesspeople, entrepreneurs, servants, preachers, and politicians all rolled into one. If we had nothing to sell, we would still have so much to offer. We have our light.

I have spent the better part of my life discovering that the key to becoming great at what we do—providing we believe in the value of what we're selling—lies exclusively in how we manage our light.

Think about what light is for a moment, what it does. Don't think of a lamp or a flashlight. That's thinking about it as an apparatus. Consider light. What does it do? What is the point of it?

When you go into a room, how do you know that it is "light"? You know because you can see the room. The more light, the more of the room you see.

Now, think about your light. When the light is on inside you, people see who you are. They can trust you because you're not hiding from them.

I know the light is on inside me because I am inspired. I can see and embrace the truth that I was made to succeed. That gives me joy, and that joy becomes visible to everyone I meet.

You've seen "light" people, haven't you? They are the ones who are comfortable in their own skin. They are always pouring into others because they themselves are satisfied. They are honest about what they don't know or can't do and they ask for help because they aren't ashamed of their frailty or their humanity.

Using the light on around you is the picture of wisdom. Wisdom is not trying to see what isn't there, or ignore what is there. Salesmen are opportunity-driven creatures. We wait for the open door, and walk through it.

If we're insisting on a path that isn't open to us, or rejecting one because the return doesn't appear to be worth our effort, then we are refusing to use the light around us. There is no sale too small, no person not worth our time.

Lastly, we have a responsibility to those who are on the path following us. Leaving the light on behind us is the debt we owe to those who went before us.

Ours is a business of giving and generosity. If we're not giving back, we're making everything we've learned invalid. We are leaving others in the dark.

Keep the light on inside you. Use the light on around you. Leave the light on behind you. At any given moment, we are managing our light in one of those ways. What does that look like in practical terms? If we all have a light, why do some of us do well while others struggle and flounder? What is the day to day working out of "light management"?

The more I sell, the more I realize that few people can really tell you *how* to sell. I spend a considerable amount of time mentoring sales professionals. I look at what they are reading and listening to. Much of it is what I read and listened to 20 or 30 years ago.

Much of it requires the salesperson to rehearse a script or memorize some affirmations. There were practical tools too, but they were written in offices by men and women who don't spend much time in the field. They were eloquent and made sense on paper, but they were difficult if not impossible to execute if a client had a need which wasn't in the list of proposed scenarios.

I am a successful, working salesman. This book was written to help other working salesmen and saleswomen uncover and/or maintain their success. It contains the practical working out of the three aforementioned rules.

What follows is the fruit of my experience in the field as a top-producing insurance agent, and an entrepreneur running a profitable business. I have coached and mentored sales professionals for many years. What I teach them is what I have written about here. I am aware that one of the challenges of a work like this is the transferability of what is being taught. Can doing what I do really make a difference in your productivity? On that front I offer no guarantees, but two facts:

1. 80% of the men and women I coach become top earners.

2. With just 20% of my time devoted to my own business and 80% focused on mentoring, I remain in the top 1/16th of 1% among agents.

My goal is to put into words the disciplines I believe are largely responsible for my success. There are 21 of these "secrets" in all. After so many years, much of what I do is done without deliberate thought, so putting it into words required me to become more self-aware than I have been in awhile. A pleasant byproduct has been the sharpening of my own skills as this book became a reality. For that I thank you.

Most of us don't have time to sit for hours and read. This chapter and the one before it are the longest in the book. From here on, the goal is not looking at information as much as perceiving it through the lens of your own passion and ideals.

It's said that a lesson "caught" is better than one merely taught. In other words, we learn best when we're *living* something instead of just reading about it. I believe that's true.

Much of what I practice daily was "caught" through a trial and error process that filtered every teaching through my experiences, understanding, and limitations. It then had to be "tailored" to fit the shape of my dreams before it could be incorporated into everyday conduct.

In other words, nothing we learn instantly transforms us. Like food or drink, we have to choose to take it in; tasting it first, then swallowing and digesting, and finally eliminating what we don't or can't use.

The following 21 secrets of my success are meant to be "fed" into your spirit, and then lived out as you come to understand them. To that end, each one is simply communicated and easy to absorb in four parts.

1. INSIGHT

2. IMAGINATION

3. INVESTIGATION

4. INITIATION

Each part urges you to actively participate in your own inner transformation instead of just observing it.

Insight challenges you to process and evaluate what you've read and restate it in language that makes sense to you. "What does this say?" and "What do I think/feel about what this says?" are the questions you should answer here.

Imagination is your opportunity to dream. It's one thing to look at an ideal and know that it worked for me. It's another to see it in operation in your own life.

Think about your life. What are the possibilities presented by what you've read? In what ways can this particular routine or ritual be worked out in your life, given your current situation and experience? Imagine what your life would look like if you were to put that discipline into action. Write down every scenario that comes into your head.

Investigation is necessary to identify the obstacles to putting what you've learned into practice. What's stopping you from incorporating this discipline? More than anywhere else be thorough and honest here. Do some soul searching. Ask someone you trust if you need help with this part.

Initiation requires you to set some goals and formulate some action steps. Simply put, goals tell you where you are going. Actions steps tell you how you will get there. Look at what you've written in your Investigation. Take one or more of the obstacles you listed, and set a goal to help you overcome it. Then create one or more rituals in your life to make room for you to reach the goals you set. Finally, what can you do or change TODAY that would weaken or eliminate an obstacle?

Change is never as simple as pretending to act out a set of values. Take advantage of every opportunity to see your life as it truly is, in view of whatever wisdom I have to offer you. Don't skip over the uncomfortable parts. You'll get the best out of this work if you bring your best into it.

The second half of this book contains a 31-day journal. It is there for you to write down your thoughts each day for one month. Some of my thoughts and reflections are there to help you focus on a specific aspect of sales and selling.

You have a decision to make now if you're going to continue with me. You could move forward as a spectator, reading about what it's like to be a number one salesman. That is a comfortable position, and safe, but I've got a better idea. Why don't you *become* Number One? Think about where you are right now? What are you hoping to accomplish over the next few years? Why not that?

I admit it won't always be comfortable or safe. Breaking through limits seldom is. Wishing for a spectacular life won't cost you anything, but actually going after it usually requires courage and sacrifice.

"Vision is not enough," said author and Czech Republic President Vaclav Havel. "It must be combined with venture. It is not enough to stare up the steps; we must step up the stairs."

My hope for you is that you would set your sights on the top, and then charge ahead. Come on. Let's venture up those stairs and into the journey of your life.

21 Secrets of a #1 Salesman

KEEP THE LIGHT ON INSIDE YOU

❧

Take a long, deep breath. All the air is coming into your lungs, moving through your body, feeding oxygen to every cell. Exhale now. Everything your cells don't need is released from you.

Keeping the light on inside you is about staying inspired. The word "inspire" literally means "inside wind." Moments are transformed into momentum as we "breathe" in the truth and let it feed us, then let go of all the lies that weigh us down and hinder our progress.

I'm not talking about rehearsing an affirmation. Thinking positive thoughts is very different from knowing the truth. Affirmation declares the value of a good life. The truth gives you the power to live a good life, even when you don't feel like it.

SECRET #1: EVERY GAME COUNTS.

SECRET #2: HALF IN = HALF WIN.

SECRET #3: STAY HUNGRY. STAY FULL.

SECRET #4: LIMITS DON'T GET A VOTE.

SECRET #5: REMEMBER WHERE YOU SLIPPED, NOT WHERE YOU FELL.

SECRET #6: LIVE EVERYDAY JUST ONCE.

SECRET #7: INVISIBLE IS NOT IMPOSSIBLE.

SECRET # 1

EVERY GAME COUNTS

❧❧

The time to start seriously thinking about ending the year on top is always at the beginning of the year.

Championships are not won on the last day of the season but all year long. Getting into the finals requires making the playoffs, but playoffs are little more than a fantasy for the team who isn't winning during the regular season.

The only people who wait until the end of the year to get excited are fans. They're not actually in the game. They are spectators watching the game, claiming allegiance to the contest without taking an active part in the battle. It's pretty easy to tell the fans from the players, even if a fan is on the field. Fans wait for things to happen. Players *make* things happen.

Good salesmen "step up" when a situation calls for it. Great ones don't have to step up because they never "let up." They see every encounter as an opportunity to shine, and they meet every experience with a sense of excitement, not just the ones that will get them over the mark.

There was a point in my career when I wanted to make a change, so I moved from Chicago to Southern California. The decision seemed like a good one when I made it, but one day it dawned on me that I had just left everything familiar to me. I had enjoyed some level of success in Chicago, but I didn't know a soul in California. I was practically starting over.

I showed up at my office gripped with fear. When my new manager asked me if I was ready for work, all I could say was, "I'm scared." I didn't even have it in me to pretend to be eager. He didn't offer me much in the way of practical direction, but what he said was what I needed to hear. "You'll be fine. Just do your job."

I was just settling in at my desk when the office assistant asked if there was someone who could take a call. A local college was about to close and the employees wanted to discuss their insurance policies with someone. It was not new business, so no one wanted to waste their time.

My manager's words were still in my head. *Do your job.* My job was to care about all people, not just the ones who could do me a favor. I took the call and made the appointment to do my job.

It turned out that everyone in the group was not only qualified to be reinsured, but doing so would work to their advantage. I ended my first week ahead of everyone at the office. There are no unimportant calls. When people matter, outcomes take care of themselves.

The time to work hard is NOW. The moment to shine is THIS MOMENT. Tomorrow is what you make of it TODAY.

INSIGHT: _____

_____

_____

_____

_____

_____

IMAGINATION: _____

_____

_____

_____

_____

_____

INVESTIGATION: _____

_____

_____

_____

_____

INITIATION: _____

_____

_____

_____

_____

_____

ADDITIONAL NOTES: _____

_____

_____

_____

_____

_____

_____

_____

_____

_____

_____

_____

_____

_____

_____

_____

_____

_____

_____

SECRET #2

HALF IN = HALF WIN

৯৯৯

You cannot tiptoe into this business of selling, and once inside, you will not stay long if you are second guessing your desire, or opting to coast rather than push yourself past your limits. You don't have to be a great salesman every day, but you should *want* to be. You don't have to step on others to be the best, but our world is no place for the half-hearted competitor.

If you're going to be in, be *all* in. Good is not good enough when you're capable of excellent. The work of your hands yields its full harvest only when you have done all that you *can* do, not all that you have decided to do, or all that you have scheduled for yourself to do.

There is a temptation to allow the expectations of others to determine how much effort we put forth. In other words, if we are better than most of the people around us—or even just perceived to be better—we see no reason to drive ourselves beyond that favorable comparison. But what if you are so much better than that?

You don't do yourself any favors committing only part

of your energy, your heart, your spirit, or your mind to the work that is before you. There is a feeling of superiority that comes with the "I can do this job with my eyes closed" attitude, especially if you see others around you struggling to do what comes so easily to you. That feeling is temporary.

Performing at less than capacity is like continuing to use an ax but never sharpening it. With time, the blade becomes duller. The trees will seem tougher and tougher to cut through, until eventually, they get the better of the woodsman more often than not. He becomes exhausted with the feeblest effort.

Commitment is the first battle to overcome and it becomes the ground upon which all other battles will be fought. Your desire has to be strong, and your labor has to continually test then best your limits. If not, your drive will become anemic and the result will be unrealized potential.

When not one part of your mind, body, or spirit is held back, you will find that the universe seems to move to support you too. People see your commitment and respond to it. Your path becomes clearer because you are not lazy on it. Opportunities become visible because you are looking for them.

Completely engage, improve steadily, and apprehend the success you were created to enjoy.

INSIGHT: _____

_____

_____

_____

_____

_____

IMAGINATION: _____

_____

_____

_____

_____

_____

INVESTIGATION: _____

_____

_____

_____

_____

INITIATION: _____

_____

_____

_____

_____

ADDITIONAL NOTES: _____

_____

_____

_____

_____

_____

_____

_____

_____

_____

_____

_____

_____

_____

_____

_____

_____

_____

_____

_____

_____

_____

_____

_____

Secret #3

Stay Hungry. Stay Full.

❦

Shakespeare's Caesar remarked, "Let me have men about me that are fat; Sleek-headed men and such as sleep o' nights: Yond Cassius has a lean and hungry look; He thinks too much: such men are dangerous."

Are you that "dangerous" person? Is your hunger visible to those around you? Does the look of you keep your competition on its toes? Do your clients know that you are not quite satisfied, and constantly thinking of new ways to do more and be more than you are?

Hunger, as I mean it here, is the hope of the spirit pressing the mind and body into unified action. When we're hungry, it is a signal that we are using up all available resources, exercising appropriate effort, and preparing ourselves to learn and grow past our present condition.

The right hunger comes from relentlessly and dependably exhausting our deposit of expertise, competence, time, and opportunities to serve. It is evidence of our readiness to go to the next level.

Hunger should never be confused with Starvation. We are

hungry when we have used up what we have. We are starving when we are focused on what we *don't* have. The starving can't hope past today. They can only dream of survival.

Nutritionists and personal trainers tell us that the healthiest people have trained themselves to efficiently use up all the food they take into their bodies. They suggest that hunger throughout the day is the best indicator that you are on the right track. They also teach us that eating—that is, feeding our hunger—throughout the day is the best way to keep our physical selves in top performance condition. Stay hungry. Stay full.

The wisdom of that is applicable to our work life. When we allow our desire for more (hungry) to drive us to learn more and sharpen our skills (full), we become better at what we do. As we continue to perform at that level, we find ourselves craving bigger and better challenges (hungry), and that drives us to acquire a higher level of proficiency (full), and so on.

When you're full, do what makes you hungry. When you're hungry, do what fills you up. There is nothing else for you to do but become excellent at those two things.

INSIGHT: _____

_____

_____

_____

_____

_____

IMAGINATION: _____

_____

_____

_____

_____

_____

_____

INVESTIGATION: _____

_____

_____

_____

_____

_____

INITIATION: _____

_____

_____

_____

_____

_____

ADDITIONAL NOTES: _____

SECRET #4

LIMITS DON'T GET A VOTE

Limits inform us. They were never meant to perform for us.

One of the hardest lessons to learn in life and sales is this: A boundary *defines* movement. It can't *direct* movement unless it has your permission.

A circus elephant is tied to a rope that limits his movement when he is young. Once he has learned that he can't go further than his tether allows, his trainer will remove the rope. The elephant is able to move where he wants to, but because he believes the attempt will end like all the others—that he will be stopped—he refuses even to attempt to journey past the length of the rope he was trained with. The limits imposed upon him now direct his behavior.

What about you?

Are you establishing goals or allowing limits to direct you? There is an easy way to know the difference. You set goals. You see limits. Goals propel you forward. Limits show you a place to stop.

Goals are a means to an end. You position them on the path

you have laid out for yourself. You decide what they are and how they fit into your plans.

A limit is a fence, something that either prohibits or discourages movement past a certain point. I love it when people ask me why, with seven number one finishes, I continue to compete. "Aren't you satisfied?" is the common query.

My answer is simple. I don't shoot for number one every year so I can be satisfied. I do it because I *am* satisfied! And because I'm satisfied, *I* decide what I will do, where I will go, and when—or if—I will stop.

A limit can only tell us what has already been done. That's important. However, in order to dream the unimaginable, we have to be willing to convert limits into goals. We do that by deciding that they are not a place, but a place on the way to a place. We let them speak to us, but not *for* us.

I left the business once during my career, because I was told that's what people my age did. It didn't matter that I still found joy in my work. Quitting on top "made sense," so I did it. That perspective was a limit, and I had given it a vote...the majority vote.

I stayed "retired" for all of two days. I still had a few more number one years ahead of me. Limits can't go beyond the reasonable. They don't walk where faith can take you. That's why they don't get to dictate my movement.

Don't let them dictate yours.

INSIGHT: _____

_____

_____

_____

_____

_____

IMAGINATION: _____

_____

_____

_____

_____

_____

INVESTIGATION: _____

_____

_____

_____

_____

INITIATION: _____

_____

_____

_____

_____

_____

ADDITIONAL NOTES: _____

_____

_____

_____

_____

_____

_____

_____

_____

_____

_____

_____

_____

_____

_____

_____

_____

_____

_____

_____

_____

SECRET #5

REMEMBER WHERE YOU SLIPPED, <u>NOT</u> WHERE YOU FELL

❧❧

If you want to get out of a hole, DON'T STUDY THE HOLE. Your setbacks are yours, but *you are not your setbacks*.

Many years ago, recovering from back to back car accidents, my productivity at work took a steep nose-dive. Physically I was in a lot of pain. Mentally, I couldn't focus. Emotionally, I was discouraged.

Eventually, I was placed on low sales probation. My manager concluded that the business had passed me by. He said he wanted me out of his office. He even suggested I quit the business and finish out my career hawking burial policies.

I was more than depressed. I was almost destroyed. My light was just about out. Everything around me said I was worthless, and I was beginning to believe it.

Eventually I told Carol what was going on and how it made me feel. I guess I was expecting some sympathy, but my wife gave me the look she gets which says what she's about to say is not up for question or discussion, so just listen.

She simply said, "Honey. That man does not know you."

It was like somebody opened a door and let in some fresh air. In that moment, I realized that I had been breathing in so many lies; I didn't even know the truth anymore. But my wife's eyes told me that she knew.

Without waiting for me to ask, she said, "You are the man I married. Focus on the things you used to do. Rehearse what you did when you were winning."

Carol is quiet, but not passive. She doesn't say a lot, but she is a deep and beautiful ocean. More than that, she has been a gift to me in every dry season of my life.

Truth isn't always visible, but it is real. It doesn't always agree with the facts, but you can stand on it. My wife taught me some things that day that I have carried with me ever since.

What were you doing before your slump or your desert season? Remind yourself that if you had one sale, you can have another. Do the things you did to get the last sale. Keep the same office hours. Make as many calls. Wear the same suit. Eat the same breakfast. If you keep a journal, go back and read it. If you can't remember what you were doing before you fell, then do what you've seen others do. Rehearse their winning behavior. Create a winning atmosphere for yourself.

Wherever you are, get up and get moving remembering this: Stumbling is not falling. Falling is not failing. Failure is not final.

It may be awhile before you come out of your hole, but it will never be your permanent address unless you choose it.

INSIGHT: _____

_____

_____

_____

_____

_____

Imagination: _____

_____

_____

_____

_____

_____

Investigation: _____

_____

_____

_____

_____

Initiation: _____

_____

_____

_____

_____

_____

ADDITIONAL NOTES: _____

_____

_____

_____

_____

_____

_____

_____

_____

_____

_____

_____

_____

_____

_____

_____

Secret #6

Live Every Day Just Once

∽ა.ჯ

We can only run so fast or go so far without falling when we're looking back at the ground we've already covered. There's no power in looking back, only in remembering as we look ahead.

What do you do with your bad weeks? Do you carry them into the next week like a shroud, announcing to the world that you have allowed your failures to define you rather than refine you?

Every day has just 24 hours in it. Depression, anger, and self-pity can stretch that time out indefinitely and cause it to intrude on the days that come after it.

I remember being very disappointed early in my career when a number of clients I had written business for started letting their policies lapse. Without telling me, they just stopped paying their premiums and then wouldn't return my phone calls.

I felt betrayed and I was very angry. I went into bitter mourning for those lost sales instead of looking for new ones, allowing myself the dangerous indulgence of feeling sorry for myself. I slept late, and sometimes, when I woke up, I didn't bother to get out of bed.

My pastor, Rev. Bronson called one day—no doubt alerted by my wife—and asked how I was.

"I'm sick," I told him.

"Get out of the bed, Sol." He acted like he hadn't heard me. I continued to make excuses, but he saw right through me and said, "Fine, then. I'm on my way over. If you're really sick, I'm going to take you to the hospital or the cemetery, but you will get out of that bed."

It would've been too embarrassing a sight, one grown man getting dragged out of bed by another (especially since I was the one getting dragged!), so I got up, got dressed and went knocking on doors. I got six sales that evening.

Yesterday is over. If it was a bad day, don't choose to live it again, or allow it to influence the next day. Do what you did on your last good day. Don't tell yourself the lie that you have to play catch up to make up for what you didn't get accomplished. Today is new. Treat it that way. Make it into whatever you want it to be.

How you feel and who you are are two very different things. Going through a day with bad feelings is like having a whiny 3-year-old in the car with you. It's okay to listen to him. Just don't let him drive.

INSIGHT: _____

_____

_____

_____

_____

_____

IMAGINATION: _____

_____

_____

_____

_____

_____

_____

INVESTIGATION: _____

_____

_____

_____

_____

_____

INITIATION: _____

_____

_____

_____

_____

_____

ADDITIONAL NOTES: _____

_____

_____

_____

_____

_____

_____

_____

_____

_____

_____

_____

_____

_____

_____

_____

_____

_____

_____

_____

_____

SECRET #7

INVISIBLE IS NOT IMPOSSIBLE

∞∞∞

What do you do with the dark?

When you are blind, which way do you go? When there's no light on the path, where do you plant your next step? When imagination fails, what do you dream? When the waters of discouragement overwhelm, how do you hope?

We're used to possibilities announcing themselves in some way. We seldom commit ourselves to anything that seems to be hiding from us. But this business is not without its "invisibility factors." How we handle them separates the merely competent among us from the truly confident.

Every move of creativity, faith, recovery, and overcoming begins with the simple act of seeing what isn't there yet. When we learn to develop our "night vision"—that is our ability to believe in things that haven't presented themselves—we open ourselves up to performance at another level.

How solid is your confidence? How convinced are you that you are where you belong, even when you're missing the mark? How good are you at encouraging yourself when empowering yourself isn't yielding tangible results? How certain are you of your ability to reach levels that no one in your industry has even come close to?

Darkness is just another place to navigate. Allowing only what you see to decide what's possible is like nailing your shoes to the ground before you attempt to fly. How high you go will be determined by the strength of your connection to the ground. How ridiculous is that?

Goethe said, "Whatever you can do, or dream you can, begin it! Boldness has genius, magic, and power in it."

The transition is one that takes us from "seeing is believing" to *"believing is seeing."* You become the vehicle of authentication by moving in the direction of the best outcome you can imagine, not the best one you've seen. Your active faith becomes the substance of what you're hoping for, and the proof that undetectable does not mean non-existent.

INSIGHT: _____

_____

_____

_____

_____

IMAGINATION: _____

_____

_____

_____

_____

_____

_____

INVESTIGATION: _____

_____

_____

_____

_____

_____

INITIATION: _____

_____

_____

_____

_____

_____

ADDITIONAL NOTES: _____

_____

_____

_____

_____

USE THE LIGHT ON AROUND YOU

❧

We are human beings. We exist; animals set apart from all others by our emotions, intellect, and will. We are also "humans being." We move through this world deliberately doing; working, loving, expressing, acting and responding to action.

Consider that between human beings and humans being, we are one other thing: We are Humans SEEING.

Standing between every dream and the execution of that dream is our vision. We can desire success, but unless we sharpen our spiritual, emotional, and mental eyesight, we will not be prepared to see it. Success won't pass us by. We will unknowingly pass by success.

Using the light on around you means having the wisdom to recognize and respond to opportunities the moment they reveal themselves. Light comes in the form of information, relationships, circumstances, and experiences. The purpose of it is to teach us, grow us, move us forward, or correct us.

SECRET #8: SHOW UP TO SHOW OFF.

SECRET #9: LATER IS TOO LATE.

SECRET #10: LISTEN WITH BOTH EYES OPEN.

SECRET #11: PLAY IT STRAIGHT.

SECRET #12: HOPE IS NOT A STRATEGIC PLAN.

SECRET #13: NO CRUMBS ON THE TABLE.

SECRET #14: GET A LIFE.

SECRET #8

SHOW UP TO SHOW OFF

❦❦

When you're winning, it's because you have some things to teach. If you're losing, it's because you have some things to learn. At any given moment, a dose of healthy competition will tell you where you stand.

Competition is good for individuals. It can push you further if you're ahead in the contest, or pull you forward if you're behind.

Winning feels great. I enjoy it, and I plan to keep doing it. I don't have to think I'm above other people, but I do allow them to push me past my own limits.

You can't be timid in this business. I think that's good advice for anyone in any business, but particularly for those of us who sell. We thrive on accomplishment. Large or small, victories are fuel for us.

Competition is also good for companies. The word literally means "to strive together," and at its root is the image of two *qualified people looking for something together.* The best companies are not full of salespeople who want to beat up on each other. The best companies employ a team of people with a common drive to succeed.

I'm reminded of the man who was coaching a kids' soccer team. One of his players kept kicking the ball down the field for the score without passing to any of his teammates.

They beat the other team, but after the game, the coach still pulled the boy aside and said, "You know, Billy, there is no 'I' in 'team.'" Billy said, "No, but there sure is one in 'WIN!'"

Never miss an opportunity to shine. How well you compete will speak to your clients louder than a hundred of your best pitches. People love to associate themselves with winners and they will give their business to someone who is at least running the race before they give it to someone too laid back to lace up his sneakers.

The pressure of competition is not always comfortable, but it's still good to have someone biting at your heels as you run. You might pay more attention to the voice inside telling you "Don't stop," if it adds, "...or they'll swallow you!"

INSIGHT: _____

_____

_____

_____

_____

_____

IMAGINATION: _____

_____

_____

_____

_____

_____

_____

INVESTIGATION: _____

_____

_____

_____

_____

_____

INITIATION: _____

_____

_____

_____

_____

_____

ADDITIONAL NOTES: _____

_____

_____

_____

_____

_____

_____

_____

_____

_____

_____

_____

_____

_____

_____

_____

_____

_____

_____

_____

_____

_____

_____

_____

_____

_____

_____

SECRET #9

LATER IS TOO LATE

Monday, Tuesday, Wednesday, Thursday, Friday, Saturday, Sunday. That's it. Those are the days of the week. There are only seven of them. No one added "Someday" while we weren't looking.

Putting off work, calls, appointments, or office management issues will kill your business and your relationships, if it doesn't kill you first.

If it weren't for the last minute, some people wouldn't get anything done. If that's you, consider this: it is impossible to effectively move forward while your back is against the wall. There is no profit in delay, no harvest if you put off planting.

Procrastination is, as one writer put it, "the art of keeping up with yesterday." I prefer to think of it as the unfortunate skill of aborting tomorrow. What opportunities never see the light of day because of the intrusion of the unfinished?

The irony is most of us put off doing work because we say we're tired or overextended. However, nothing is as exhausting to the human spirit and mind as an uncompleted task hanging overhead.

When there is work to be done, separate it into two categories: 1) **things which have to be put on a schedule**, and 2) **things that don't have to be on a schedule**. Once you've put everything from the first list on your calendar, turn your attention to the second list.

Again, put each of these items into one of two categories: 1) **what can be put off forever**, and 2) **what cannot be put off at all**. You are bound by just those two options. If you think a task is somewhere in between, put it in the category that best fits it.

Once you're finished, schedule every item which cannot be put off at all. If it is worth doing, it is worth scheduling.

Now take the "what can be put off forever" list, and THROW IT AWAY. Why would you occupy your mind with things you can put off forever? If knowing that an item will be forgotten bothers you, schedule it. Make a habit of doing what needs to be done no sooner, and especially no later than it is able to be done.

"Later" is not a setting on anyone's clock. Using it is like paying for a ticket on a plane bound for "someplace."

INSIGHT: _____

_____

_____

_____

_____

IMAGINATION: _____

_____
_____
_____
_____
_____
_____

INVESTIGATION: _____
_____
_____
_____
_____
_____

INITIATION: _____
_____
_____
_____
_____
_____

ADDITIONAL NOTES: _____
_____

THE SECRET LIFE OF A # 1 SALESMAN

_____

_____

_____

_____

_____

_____

_____

_____

_____

_____

_____

_____

_____

_____

_____

_____

_____

_____

_____

_____

_____

_____

Secret # 10

Listen With Both Eyes Open

❧

Selling is not talking, it's listening, and not just with your ears.

The best salesmen give people their **undivided attention.** When it comes to meeting someone's needs, there is no such thing as "small talk." It's all big and meaningful if you know what to listen for and how to listen for it.

Words don't mean anything apart from people, and what people *don't* say is often more telling and useful than what they do say. Absorbing that truth transforms your perspective and your performance.

People have a right to be heard. How many times have we, well, *heard* that? It isn't actually true, though, not even in the freest country.

Being heard is not a right. A right is something you can demand and enforce. You can't demand that a person hear you, and there is no one to make someone hear you, or punish them if they won't hear you.

Hearing is a *gift* and it can only be offered to you by a person who has chosen to listen to you. The art of listening requires that you see three things before you try to process one word of conversation.

First, you have to **see a person's worth**. If you have ever had an exchange with someone you didn't like or were angry with, you know that "tuning out" is a sure sign that you have little or no respect for what they're saying. If you find yourself talking down to a client, thinking negatively about them, or if your priority is simply to lead them to your close, you're in danger of missing their true value.

When you value a person, you value what they have to say. You shouldn't be doing all the talking in a meeting. If you are, the odds are you will not get the sale, or you will not get the sale you could've gotten if you had listened more. Ask good questions, and then wait for good answers. Don't lead your client. Follow him.

Second, you have to **see a person's actual need under their stated needs.** Behind every sale is a relationship. The average person has already made up his mind about a product before you show up. The question is less often, "Do I want this?" than "Do you care about me, and can I trust you to care about me after you get what you want?" If your answer to that question is no, your big smile, glib talk, and Sunday manners won't matter. They will hear the truth loud and clear.

Finally, you have to **see your entire person as an instrument of hearing.** Make eye contact. Close your mouth. Focus your mind. Don't think of answers while someone is talking. Turn your body toward the discussion, not away from it.

Giving someone your undivided attention is an act of service. For the length of your time together, you are not your own. An experience with you should leave a person believing that you heard their words, but that you also "discovered" them like hidden treasure…and you have.

INSIGHT: _____

_____

_____

_____

_____

_____

IMAGINATION: _____

_____

_____

_____

_____

_____

INVESTIGATION: _____

_____

_____

_____

_____

_____

INITIATION: _____

_____

_____

_____

_____

_____

ADDITIONAL NOTES: _____

_____

_____

_____

_____

_____

_____

_____

_____

_____

_____

_____

_____

_____

_____

SECRET #11

PLAY IT STRAIGHT

❧❧

Doing a thing right is not nearly as important as doing the right thing. People will forgive you for just about anything... except lying to them.

Like every other skill, honesty should be practiced until we become excellent at it. Our customers should be given opportunities to believe us again and again until they come to expect it.

It takes less time and effort to do things truthfully than it does to explain why you didn't, and it will cost you less in the long run. Nothing is harder to get back than lost trust.

People are open to doing business with us if we're knowledgeable, efficient, and we give them their money's worth. However, we don't actually get the business until and unless we persuade them of our ability to deliver on our promises. Even then, the deal is not completely sealed until we actually begin to deliver.

Don't make false promises just to get a sale. Every piece of bait you dangle and eventually switch chips away at a person's confidence in you. If you're paying attention, you'll see the exact moment when he decides you are no longer believable. It may be too late for him to change his mind about the current sale, but you will have lied your way out of repeat and referral business.

Don't claim to know more than you actually do. There's no crime in not knowing, only in not learning. My first sale was to a man who appreciated my honesty in telling him I could not compute his rate without help.

On the other end of the spectrum, **don't withhold knowledge, information, or options.** It's good for our ego to be the smartest person in the room. There is something about doling out information that gives us the illusion that we are in control; that every variable of a sale is in our hands and under our influence.

The truth is believability is a function of credibility, and credibility comes from our being truthful. If we don't empower people with what we know, they will begin to feel manipulated or condescended to. They will become suspicious of us, and they would have every right to be. It is impossible to build anything lasting on a lopsided foundation.

When people see that you are willing to tell them what you know—that you trust *them*—it inspires them, gives them a sense of security, and draws them closer to you.

Honesty, loyalty, integrity, and faithfulness are indispensable if you want a career in sales and not just a job.

INSIGHT: _____

_____

_____

_____

_____

_____

IMAGINATION: _____

_____

_____

_____

_____

_____

INVESTIGATION: _____

_____

_____

_____

_____

_____

INITIATION: _____

_____

_____

_____

_____

_____

ADDITIONAL NOTES: _____

_____

_____

_____

_____

_____

_____

_____

_____

_____

_____

_____

_____

_____

_____

_____

_____

_____

_____

_____

SECRET # 12

HOPE IS NOT A STRATEGIC PLAN

❧❧

There are explanations for failure, but never for failing to prepare. Wanting to know how to swim will not save you when you're drowning. Wishing you had gas in your tank will not help you on a long stretch of highway.

There is an old saying that we should always "keep our eyes on the prize." I think a better idea is to keep your <u>heart</u> on the prize, your <u>eyes</u> on the road, your <u>hand</u> on the plow, and your <u>mind</u> on the work.

You'll never reap a harvest if, instead of laboring, you're watching the clouds for signs of rain.

Nothing worth having is gotten without sacrifice and cost. If success is good enough for you, then you have to be good enough for it. That means planning your work and working your plan.

There's nothing wrong with making plans if a way becomes clear to you. If the way is very steep, hard, or too dark, sometimes a plan is the only thing that gives you the courage to move forward.

Twelve days before the end of a year, I was 135th in line for the President's Trophy, Prudential Financial's award for the number one agent. My wife believed it was my year to win, and she told me so.

135th place with 12 days left to work in the year. I needed a plan. We got 90 apps, made a lot of phone calls, set dozens of appointments, and traveled to 22 cities in 11 days. That trophy didn't come to us; we had to go get it, moment by moment. I kept my eyes on the prize, but my mind was fixed on our plan, and my hands remained firmly on the work I had to do.

Plans should be specific. They're not etched in stone, but they aren't written on water either. The willingness to do what it takes to get what you want is the only proof you have that your desire is real.

Set goals. Learn all there is to know about where you're going. Share your plans with people who can help you make them happen. Chart your progress and share that too.

Don't wait for your life to become amazing. Make it so.

INSIGHT: _____

_____

_____

_____

_____

_____

IMAGINATION: _____

_____

_____

_____

_____

_____

_____

INVESTIGATION: _____

_____

_____

_____

_____

_____

INITIATION: _____

_____

_____

_____

_____

_____

ADDITIONAL NOTES: _____

_____

_____

SECRET # 1 3

NO CRUMBS ON THE TABLE

ॐ৯ॐ

I used to belong to a small study group made up of top producers from all over the state where I lived. We met monthly to share best practices and encourage one another.

We believed that no client was too big to go after, and no business was too small to turn away. Our mantra was "leave no crumbs on the table." Looking back, I realize that ideal has characterized my entire career.

I was cold calling one day and I met a woman who wanted someone to come out and talk to her about getting some insurance. I was still pretty new in the business and every lead was exciting to me. However, when I asked the agents in the office for directions to the part of town she lived in, they said it was a dangerous neighborhood, and not to go alone.

Cabrini Greens was a slum on the south side of Chicago. It was famous for its crime, drug trade, and gang problem. The sanitation department had stopped collecting the garbage there and at its worst, it was piled five stories high and could be smelled from blocks away.

No one in the office would go with me. But I decided to

keep the appointment anyway. I got there late at night. The elevator in the building wasn't working, so I felt my way up the dark stairs, kicking trash and trying not to notice the rustling sounds around me.

The woman was a little surprised to see me. She said whenever she told people where she lived, they wouldn't show up, and stopped taking her calls. I was so glad that I had kept the appointment. She was married with two children; a very nice lady, just looking to make her family a little more secure.

We chatted for awhile, and she bought a policy. I was so grateful I could help her; I practically skipped down the stairs when I left.

A few weeks later, her husband was attacked coming home from work. He was robbed and murdered right outside their apartment building.

What if I had waited for someone to go with me to Cabrini Green? Would I have ever gotten there? What if I had decided that one small piece of business in a poor community wasn't worth my time?

I personally delivered that woman's settlement check. She was solemn as she looked at it, but I saw something else too. She could move from this place. Maybe her kids could go to college. Nothing would return the husband to his wife or the father to his children. But life without him would not be without hope.

She looked up at me and said, "God sent you to me that night." I know she was right, and every once in awhile, especially when I'm tired and I wonder if what I do is worth doing, I think of her.

INSIGHT: _____

_____

_____

_____

_____

_____

IMAGINATION: _____

_____

_____

_____

_____

_____

INVESTIGATION: _____

_____

_____

_____

_____

INITIATION: _____

_____

_____

_____

_____

_____

ADDITIONAL NOTES: _____

_____

_____

_____

_____

_____

_____

_____

_____

_____

_____

_____

_____

_____

_____

SECRET #14

GET A LIFE

❧❧

What is there besides your work? Who are you apart from it? What do you long for that has nothing to do with it?

The great failure in life is not to be without money, position, or power. The great failure is to be without the incorruptible treasures of peace, joy, courage, and gratitude. It is tragic to simply earn a living and have no yearning for things that can't be bought, borrowed, or made with human hands.

Your actions express your priorities, specifically how you spend your time and what you do with your money. What are you giving time to and what, or whom, are you taking time from? Does your money draw you nearer to or separate you from those closest to you? When you are the success you desire to be, will they have more or less of what they desire from you?

You are more than your numbers, quotas, and trophies. You must reach for more than rewards and praise. If you are too busy to care about someone or be cared for by someone, YOU ARE TOO BUSY.

Establishing a healthy existence apart from your career is

critical, especially if you've set your sights on being number one. If there is no one motivating you to climb higher and become a better person, success will be empty at best.

What kind of parent do you hope your children grow up to be? Be that parent. Marriage is not so much finding the right person as it is *being* the right person. Become the husband or wife you want to have.

Is your family on your schedule or do they get what's left of you after the world has wrung every smile and chuckle out of you? Are you cheating on your spouse with your job?

If you were dying tomorrow, would you be satisfied with how you have lived? Would the people around you agree with your assessment?

Regardless of the amount of time it takes up, work should always be a means to an end. Work is a vehicle that exists to help you make space for your priorities. Be grateful for it. Respect its power to provide. Allow it to refine and transform you, but always remember what matters most.

The length of time you devote to your work will have the most value if you have devoted your heart to the depth of your relationships.

INSIGHT: _____

_____

_____

_____

_____

IMAGINATION: _____

_____

_____

_____

_____

_____

_____

INVESTIGATION: _____

_____

_____

_____

_____

INITIATION: _____

_____

_____

_____

_____

_____

ADDITIONAL NOTES: _____

_____

_____

_____

_____

_____

_____

_____

_____

_____

_____

_____

_____

_____

_____

_____

_____

_____

_____

_____

_____

_____

_____

_____

LEAVE THE LIGHT ON BEHIND YOU

❧❧

You are a gift. Whether you know it or not, you are on this earth for a reason. You're in this business for a reason.

You were designed to matter to others, to factor into their lives and if possible, change them for the better.

Ours is a ministry of offering up whatever light we have been privileged to have or use. In doing that, we become the very light we bestow. When we teach what we have learned, we shine. We sacrifice ourselves to others because we know that we were once rescued from darkness.

Someone needs you. Someone needs to know what only you can tell them, see what no one else but you can show them. Someone is bound by things you've been liberated from. Someone is in a pit you once fell into yourself.

If it were just a matter of giving time, resources, and advice, there would be nothing life-altering about it. If however, your giving is the outworking of the gift of yourself, then you have truly imparted something of enduring value. At the end of the day, our job is to let people know that they are not alone. We leave the light on for them not just to help them see, but so they can see that we are with them on their journey.

SECRET # 1 5: YOUR CHOICE IS YOUR VOICE.

SECRET # 1 6: LET THEM SEE YOU SWEAT.

SECRET # 1 7: WORK LEAN AND CLEAN.

SECRET #18: MAKE ROOM UNDER YOUR WINGS.

SECRET #19: THE BEST GET REST.

SECRET #20: SACRIFICE IS SACRED.

SECRET #21: LIVE TO TELL YOUR STORY.

SECRET #15

YOUR CHOICE IS YOUR VOICE

◈◈

People may or may not believe what you say, but they will always believe what you do. The sale is not always given to the glib or swift of tongue. It is most often won by the man or woman who, more than just talking a good game, actually walks the talk.

Integrity is bringing what I do and what I say in line with what's right. It is a word that, literally rendered, paints a picture of "wholeness, soundness, and perfect condition."

Our integrity is the one tool we can never part with. People buy our promises as well as our products, and trust our word along with our wares. If we tell them that we're in the business of serving and caring, then show up late or cancel appointments, we bring the quality of everything associated with us into question.

Conversely, we can, through our behavior, increase our credibility and encourage others to trust us simply by doing what we say we're going to do, without delay and without excuse.

We can cement a declaration that we care about people by making an extra effort on their behalf, or by making sacrifices

THE SECRET LIFE OF A #1 SALESMAN

for them.

Showing up on time and prepared to work speaks volumes to a person who has asked you to mentor him. He knows that your expressed desire to help him isn't just lip service.

Your friends and the people you choose to associate yourself with is a commentary on your confidence (or lack of same) and your relationship needs. Your level of fitness, grooming, and even your phone manner will articulate something about you.

Who you are is what you do, for better or worse. The good news is you have a choice about whether it will be for better or worse.

First, take a look at what you say and what you do for any inconsistencies. Where you find yourself acting in a way that is not in line with what you say, examine what you believe—really believe at your core—about the issue.

Use your head. Think about the logic of what you believe. Does it make sense? If it doesn't, what are some of the deeper emotional issues causing your unreasonable beliefs? Don't be afraid to look there. We can't control how we feel, even when what we feel is not grounded in sound logic. What we can do is be aware of and move to correct belief systems which can cause us to falter despite our best efforts to succeed.

The key to developing integrity is self-awareness. The more you know about yourself, the better equipped you'll be to give yourself authentically to others.

INSIGHT: _____

_____
_____
_____
_____
_____

IMAGINATION: _____
_____
_____
_____
_____
_____
_____

INVESTIGATION: _____
_____
_____
_____
_____
_____

INITIATION: _____
_____
_____

_____

_____

_____

ADDITIONAL NOTES: _____

_____

_____

_____

_____

_____

_____

_____

_____

_____

_____

_____

_____

_____

_____

_____

_____

_____

_____

SECRET #16

LET THEM SEE YOU SWEAT

❧❧

Show me the salesman who already knows everything, and I'll show you the last person in the world you want to give your business to. Show me one who never needs help, and I'll show you one who isn't growing. Show me the salesman who doesn't struggle or has never been afraid, and I'll show you somebody who will never be any better than he is right now.

Learning curves, personal challenges and obstacles to overcome are all a given part of our profession. They are the markers of growth and transformation. Without them, we don't change and we never learn to push past our limits.

However, more important than coming to the end of our self-assurance and our capabilities, is letting others see us reach that point. When our vulnerabilities are exposed—when we're forced to admit our ignorance and inability—we become accountable to the people around us for our improvement.

Our reflex is not to declare our ignorance, but to cover it up with false confidence, not to reach out for help, but to hide until help comes to us in secret. That is pride, and indulging it keeps us in bondage to our fear.

Asking for help, educating ourselves, and allowing our weakness to be visible to others liberates us from the fear of being "found out."

We are human. We are not always in control. Sometimes we need help. Admitting that puts us in a position to receive what we need.

There is no shame in finitude. If we're not being stretched, we're not growing. Comfort and grand conquest seldom go hand in hand.

Finally, reaching our limits in full view of others lets them know that obstacles cannot keep us from moving forward, darkness cannot keep us from finding our way, and that our greatest weakness often leads us to moments of great strength.

Show me a salesman with the courage to learn what he doesn't know, ask for help when he needs it, and contend with his weaknesses. Then I'll show you a salesman with the confidence to win, and the character to light the way for others.

INSIGHT: _____

_____

_____

_____

_____

IMAGINATION: _____

_____

_____

_____

_____

_____

_____

INVESTIGATION: _____

_____

_____

_____

_____

_____

INITIATION: _____

_____

_____

_____

_____

ADDITIONAL NOTES: _____

_____

_____

SECRET # 17

FLY LEAN AND CLEAN

✥

Two things cause a plane to fly lower and slower: dirt on the outside and weight on the inside. There are two things which cause us to fly lower and slower: bitterness and unforgiveness.

Bitterness is what happens when we define a circumstance by its ugliness. Unforgiveness is deciding that a person or a relationship should be defined only in terms of how it hurt us.

I can be bitter about a sale that went wrong, a string of bad weeks, my home life, changes at the office. Anything that leaves a bad taste has the potential to become bitterness if I choose to focus on the taste.

Sometimes an encounter with a person leaves me feeling bad. Unforgiveness keeps a record of those feelings and lets them become the substance of that association.

At the bottom of bitterness and my unwillingness to forgive are two ideas. Bitterness declares that I deserved better from a situation. Unforgiveness is my declaration that I am better than another person.

That first idea gives us permission to carry our sourness around with us. We've all seen bitter people. They can't enjoy anything fully because bitterness becomes the lens through which they see every experience. It's like wearing a pair of dirty glasses. The look of everything is transformed by them.

We decide not to forgive people who have wronged us (or who appear to have), as a way to rid ourselves of the burden of the relationship. It's an act of self-protection that seems reasonable at first glance, even wise. We think we are making ourselves free, but the opposite actually happens.

Unforgiveness is a weight on the heart. The place that a person occupies inside us doesn't disappear because we got hurt. Unforgiveness is just an anchor we attach to our feelings to keep them from rising to the surface.

Unforgiveness makes us heavier, not lighter. Bitterness makes things cloudier, not clearer. Neither of them are indulgences we can afford if we want to move fast or fly high.

We can rid ourselves of the poison of bitterness by learning whatever lessons we can from a particular situation, then acknowledging the resilience that brought us through it. Bitter circumstances can make us better if we let them.

Forgiveness is not a decision to forget an offense. You can't forgive what you won't remember anymore than you can heal a wound you won't admit to having. Rather it is choosing to remember a person in a different way, a humbler way.

If people only cared about us when we treated them well, how could we trust them with the awful parts of us. Forgiving a person means offering up the grace that we hope will be offered up to us when it gets out that we ourselves are not perfect.

INSIGHT: _____

_____

_____

_____

_____

_____

IMAGINATION: _____

_____

_____

_____

_____

_____

INVESTIGATION: _____

_____

_____

_____

_____

INITIATION: _____

_____

_____

_____

_____

_____

ADDITIONAL NOTES: _____

_____

_____

_____

_____

_____

_____

_____

_____

_____

_____

_____

_____

_____

_____

_____

_____

_____

_____

SECRET # 18

MAKE ROOM UNDER YOUR WINGS

⊷⊷

The greatest reward you will ever receive in our line of work is not a number one trophy. It will be, if you are fortunate enough to earn it, the opportunity to nurture others. Making your wisdom and experience available for them will fill you in ways that trophies and awards can't begin to.

You will be surprised at how much you have to teach others, especially if you look for men and women struggling with the same challenges you have overcome. You do work harder when you have others depending on you, but you also learn more and stay sharper too.

When Prudential was looking for mentors, I volunteered right away. They were shocked when I asked for the company's lowest performers.

I wanted the men and women who were discouraged and damaged. I asked them to give me as many tired, poor, whipped and weary agents as they could get their hands on. They thought I was crazy. They said I wouldn't have any time to work on my own business. I was willing to take that chance. It was a decision that would transform me and the way I did my job.

I gave them my light to see by. I walked with them, talked to them, and encouraged them with the truth of my own experiences. They saw my strengths and I showed them my weaknesses. If they asked me questions I didn't know the answer to, we learned together, and got better together.

I'm not the most educated man, but I do know that I made a difference. 80% of them became top producers. Many of them still are. There is barely a hint of the timid, insecure and uncertain men and women who originally came to me. I am proud to call them my friends and my peers.

Making room in your life to teach someone will only make you better at what you do. A candle loses nothing when it lights another candle. In fact there is twice as much light.

Oh, and the other agents were right...sort of. It is true that as a mentor, I only spend 20% of my time focused on my own business.

That's okay. I'm still on top, only now I have company.

INSIGHT: _____

_____

_____

_____

_____

_____

IMAGINATION: _____

_____
_____
_____
_____
_____
_____

INVESTIGATION: _____
_____
_____
_____
_____
_____

INITIATION: _____
_____
_____
_____
_____
_____
_____

ADDITIONAL NOTES: _____
_____

SECRET #19

THE BEST GET REST

❧❧❧

There is nothing impressive in busy-ness. It's usually a signal to others that you are unorganized and desperate. Working harder and faster just makes a man tired, and tired men make mistakes.

The great misconception about work is that its opposite is rest. The thinking is that you can only rest if you're not working, and vice versa. The truth could not be further from that idea.

Rest can mean a lot of things; to sleep, to remain somewhere, an intermission between movements. Whatever rest is, it is NOT just doing nothing.

Rest is having the freedom to do only what the moment requires and nothing more. We rest *in our work*. Rest is active, and it requires our engagement. Most important, it is a function of order. It is best when we are at our best.

Workaholics don't rest. They are usually too wrapped up in their own importance to believe that there are moments in a day that they are not required to frantically participate in.

Do others see you anxious and running around like there

aren't enough hours in a day? Your work will only be as good as your rest. If you're too busy to get rest, then 100% of the time, the problem is you're too busy.

On the other extreme, lazy people can't rest. They have too many moments worth of things they didn't do yesterday crowding in on the things they have to do today.

Rest is as important to what we do as the assignments we have, the calls we have to make, or the appointments we have to keep. Rest and work are like the shore and the sea. Ships travel far on the sea, but repairs and restocking happen on the shore.

Your ability and willingness to rest is a function of the level of respect you have for what you do. Do you respect time, set priorities, people, and education? Do you have a healthy respect for your own needs, desires, and purpose? That is just as important

Work. Rest. Do them both and you will succeed.

INSIGHT: _____

_____

_____

_____

_____

_____

IMAGINATION: _____

_____

_____

_____

_____

_____

_____

Investigation: _____

_____

_____

_____

_____

Initiation: _____

_____

_____

_____

_____

_____

Additional Notes: _____

_____

_____

SECRET #20

SACRIFICE IS SACRED

ᘓᘔ

Anything worth having is going to cost somebody something. That is a good thing, because the willingness to pay the cost confirms its value to you and affirms it to others.

Sacrifice is a theme that will run throughout your life if you have any dreams at all of personal, professional, or relational success. The forms of sacrifice are many and varied, and if we live normally, we inevitably find ourselves being required to make at least a few.

Sacrifice is usually seen in terms of how it diminishes what we have, but in order for it to be truly appreciated as a necessary and worthy part of life—one that adds value—we have to see it from another perspective.

More than just an action or a behavior, sacrifice is a posture, an attitude we choose to adopt that defines and directs our behavior. A sacrificial posture makes us open to unselfish ways like giving up our need to win an argument, offering a little extra time to a difficult client, spending a free evening working with a struggling colleague, or exercising more to please a spouse.

If you have or know of good, healthy, lasting relationships, sacrifice has had a part in them. If you have seen someone realize a lifelong dream, you won't have to look too far back to see sacrifice.

There is very little I would not give up for my family, and when I look back at my career, I know that they have sacrificed a lot for me.

Our clients should know that they are worth a sacrifice of time and effort. It's worth the financial sacrifice to widen our knowledge base.

There are two kinds of gratitude in the world: the kind we feel when we receive, and the deeper more lasting kind we experience when we give ourselves or our substance for a greater cause.

Sacrifice is a way and a means to fulfillment. It completes us, and cements our place in the world.

INSIGHT: _____

_____

_____

_____

_____

IMAGINATION: _____

_____

_____

_____

_____

_____

_____

Investigation: _____

_____

_____

_____

_____

Initiation: _____

_____

_____

_____

_____

Additional Notes: _____

_____

_____

_____

_____

_____

_____

_____

_____

_____

_____

_____

_____

_____

_____

_____

_____

_____

_____

_____

_____

_____

_____

_____

_____

_____

_____

_____

SECRET #21

LIVE TO TELL YOUR STORY

⤠⤟

The best thing you have to offer the world is you. In your story, there is a unique message for the world, if you are willing to tell it.

In your story, there are obstacles that did not kill you, and lives which are better because of you. In your story, someone may learn that life is an adventure, or that love conquers all.

When someone asks me how I handle the fear of rejection, I tell them the story of how I proposed to my wife the day I met her every day for 85 days after until she finally said yes to me. She's really the reason I know I can sell.

If I want to encourage you to think on your feet, I go back to a cold Chicago morning in a parking lot.

My appointment didn't answer the door after I rode the bus all the way out to see him. I saw a man getting out of his car. I decided to talk to him so my trip wouldn't be a total waste.

I asked him if he wanted some insurance. He said he was just getting home from being out all night. He had an angry wife upstairs and he wasn't thinking about buying insurance.

I said, "If she's really mad, maybe you need somebody to go

with you." He thought that was a pretty good idea.

We got inside. He introduced me to his wife and went to the back of the apartment. I could tell she wanted me to leave so she could have it out with him. I was certain he wouldn't be resting too long after I left. Then I thought of something.

"Does he do this often, you know, staying out all night?" I asked. She told me he did. "Well, maybe you should have some insurance on him."

I don't know if he ever stayed out all night again, but I do know she always paid her premium on time.

When you live to tell your story, you authenticate and declare the beauty of your whole life, not just the comfortable parts of it. With your story, you can encourage, strengthen, teach, or coach. You can smooth out a rough place, bring peace to a fearful place, or create room in a tight place.

Who are you? What kind of light do you have to give to the world? Take time to mine the collection of moments concerning you for the jewels of your life narrative. You are a treasure worth discovering, a beautiful story unfolding.

INSIGHT: _____

_____

_____

_____

_____

IMAGINATION: _____

_____
_____
_____
_____
_____
_____

INVESTIGATION: _____
_____
_____
_____
_____
_____

INITIATION: _____
_____
_____
_____
_____
_____

ADDITIONAL NOTES: _____
_____

_____
_____
_____
_____
_____
_____
_____
_____
_____
_____
_____
_____
_____
_____
_____
_____
_____
_____
_____
_____
_____
_____
_____
_____

31 Days of Wisdom

DAY ONE

*"Those who say it can't be done are usually
interrupted by others doing it."*
–James A. Baldwin

Suppose I told you that all of the tools necessary to transform you into a top producing salesman are right under the chair you're sitting in? You might check immediately for them, providing you believed me. It would certainly be worth the effort.

If I said that everything you need to succeed is a mere ten blocks away from where you stand, and I told you exactly where to go, again, you would probably make whatever effort was necessary to take possession of such a treasure. In fact, knowing that the implements of success were not only available but accessible might even lead you to believe that success was your divine destiny.

Well, I should tell you that the tools are not ten blocks away. And they are not under your seat either. They're actually closer. Every tool you need to build a bridge from standard to stellar is actually in your seat.

It all begins and ends with you. You've brought everything you're going to need for your journey to a brilliant tomorrow in a vessel that is as close as your own mirror. The only question is: Are you willing to make whatever effort is necessary to put to use what you already have?

DAY TWO

"It is our character that supports the promise of our future - far more than particular government programs or policies."
—William Bennett

Everyone leaves a legacy, whether they intend to or not. The second you encounter another person, who you are—good and bad—calls out to them. What are we saying through our work, in our relationships, and with our actions?

I realize that in any given moment, I have only one gift to offer, and that is the good fruit of my **character.** It is the one thing that I believe has marked every success in my life, and has worked every failure for my good.

Character is that internal sense of "rightness" which shapes our external interaction with the world. It draws us continually to wise and virtuous decisions, keeping us honest in word and honorable in deed. Character is more than a reputation. It is the revelation of one's true self; who we really are irrespective of appearances.

With character, all things become possible. Without it, even God can't do His best in me, for me, or through me. I have not been a perfect agent, husband, father, friend, or salesman. But if character is cultivated in me, I will daily strive to be excellent at all of those things.

DAY THREE

"If your energy is as boundless as your ambition, total commitment
may be a way of life you should seriously consider."
–Dr. Joyce Brothers

_____
_____
_____
_____
_____
_____
_____
_____
_____
_____
_____
_____
_____
_____

Selling doesn't begin with a call. It begins with a commitment.

Simply defined, a **commitment** is a pledge. When you commit yourself to someone, you pledge yourself to them in some way, for a specific purpose.

If we look at the actual construction of the word, we find images that enrich and enhance our understanding. The word "commitment" is made up of two words, "*com*," which means "with" and "*mittere*," which is French for "to send." So to be committed to something or someone means literally "to be sent with" them.

It's important that you see the picture here. Commitment means to *send* with, not to *go* with. When you go, the choice of path is yours. When you are sent, the path is chosen for you. Commitment is always about more than just your needs and your desires.

When we are truly committed, our success or failure at any endeavor is influenced and at times determined by the health or frailty of what or whom we're committed to. If I am sent with you, that means I go where you go, and whatever happens, happens to both of us.

There is a wonderful treasure hidden in this idea: If I am committed to you, then making sure you prosper ensures my own prosperity.

DAY FOUR

*"You can start right where you stand and apply the habit of going
the extra mile by rendering more service and better service than
you are now being paid for."*
—Napoleon Hill

_____

_____

_____

_____

_____

_____

_____

_____

_____

_____

_____

_____

_____

_____

_____

If necessity is the mother of invention, creativity is its father.

When I started marketing life insurance to people in ministry, I found out quickly that there were only a few products that fit my customers' specific needs. That didn't mean Prudential Financial didn't have what they required. It just meant that I had to care enough about the client to work a little harder.

I customized insurance and financial plans for them by piecing together different parts from a variety of products. I would become one of the chief architects of a line of ministry and nonprofit products and services still in use today.

Creativity born out of commitment is never a waste of time. Every extra mile I walked prepared me to better serve the next pastor or spiritual leader. Now these great men and women happily offer to help me reach my goals. They readily refer their friends to me, because they trust my concern for them. I have made their success my business. So they have made my success their business.

DAY FIVE

"People get work done, not buildings, not staffs in a generic sense, and not plans, but people."
–Colin Powell

Customers aren't "sales," "prospects," "aps," or "numbers." They are single mothers, husbands, students, widows, preachers, secretaries, and grandparents. When it comes to them, we are not "agents" or "reps." We are men and women who should always remember to care. We should never forget that we too can be fearful, irresponsible, slow to respond, uncertain, and insecure about our futures. It should genuinely bother us when individuals can't or won't choose to improve, protect, or add value to their lives with our products or services. I have been grieved by men or women who are so deep in debt that they can't afford life in-surance.

How many calls have you passed on to others because they didn't promise you any sizeable return? Those weren't "calls" you gave away. Those were *people*.

DAY SIX

"Most of us serve our ideals by fits and starts. The person who makes a success of living is one who sees his goal steadily and aims for it unswervingly. That's dedication."
–Cecil B. DeMille

The counterfeits of dedication are **complacency** and **control.**

You know you are complacent and not dedicated when you find yourself on a path with no end in mind. Notice I didn't say "no end in sight." We don't always need to see the end of a road. We only need to see enough of it to take the next step.

No end in *mind* means you're not really concerned where you end up tomorrow, as long as you are comfortable today. You really have no way of knowing if the path you're on is leading you closer to or further away from success.

Complacent people can appear dedicated. "Acceptable" is the armor they wear into the field. They are indistinguishable from the true soldiers until and unless the work gets hard and they are threatened with eviction from their comfort zone. Then they must choose to commit themselves to a battle or surrender and walk away.

Controlling people, on the other hand, have an end in mind, but no preference about the path it takes to get there, or concern for the people they hurt on the way.

They seem dedicated until circumstances run contrary to their pre-set ideals, plans, and opinions. When that happens, controlling outcomes becomes the priority. They submit the needs of others to their own egos, and service usually gets sacrificed along with long-term results.

A controlling agent talks.

A dedicated agent listens. A controlling agent pushes. A dedicated one guides.

Leave your own agenda at the door. Hear what the *client* says his or her needs are. Get all the facts and learn how to analyze the details. Know whom you're talking to before you offer specific help. When people know that you are dedicated enough to really listen to them, they will show you how to close the sale.

DAY SEVEN

"Real education should educate us out of self and into something far finer; into a selflessness which links us to all humanity."
–Nancy Astor

What is in your head? How much do you know about what you do? More importantly, what are you doing with what you know?

What's in your heart should be constant. Success or slump, your commitment should be strong. Your concern for people should not waver. Your emotions should be engaged. But what's in your head should be constantly increasing and expanding.

Learning is as much a part of what we do as earning, and access to the most cutting-edge resources and advanced information can bring greater rewards than a met quota.

Professionally, we owe it to the people we serve to know as much as we can about what's available to them. I am constantly looking for new ways to inform my customers. I do whatever it takes to stay informed. When I looked for ways to strengthen the niche I had created serving men and women in ministry, the resources I found and used helped direct and deepen me as a salesman.

Personally, we are obligated to tell people everything we know, so that they can help us become better providers for them. I have seen agents lose clients because they were doling out information like they were giving food to a baby. They thought the only way to keep a client was to know more than he did...until another agent was generous enough to teach.

If you're not learning more about what you do,

how to do it, and just plain old human nature, you're in danger of becoming unnecessary. Worse than that, if you're not using what you learn to educate others, you're in danger of becoming irrelevant.

DAY EIGHT

"We make a living by what we get, but we make a life by what we give."
—*Winston Churchill*

I believe there is a big difference between mere achievement and true success. What most of the world shoots for is achievement; a standard marked by awards and accolades.

Authentic success, while it includes awards, extends to the rewards found in allowing your accomplishments to light the way for those who are following you. You can do more good in two months by becoming interested in other people than you can in two years by trying to get other people interested in doing good for you.

Reaching back to help someone is our obligation in this business. Honoring that obligation is the only way to repay those who went before us, who lit paths we couldn't see, and set records for us to challenge.

No one advances holding onto his own coattails. Those men and coming behind us need something they can only get from us. They need a living witness. They need an "overcomer" who can show them how to "come over" whatever they're struggling with.

They need more folks to speak into their lives who have authority, wisdom and a few battle scars. They need to be encouraged by those of us who remember what it feels like to be discouraged.

DAY NINE

"Riches, mediocrity and poverty begin in the mind…Reality is the mirror of your thoughts. Choose well what you put in front of the mirror."
—Remez Sassoon

Your mind can be your greatest help or your greatest hindrance. What you think about a circumstance, a situation, or a client, can mean the difference between confident pursuit and half-hearted effort. Your thoughts can defeat you before you sit down for that first appointment. But they can also bulldoze you past discouragement and disappointment.

It's important to understand that before others can be sold on what you are offering, you have to be sold on yourself. You have to know who you are and be able to express that to them.

More than 70% of communication is non-verbal.

People focus more on what you do than on what you say. If you meet a prospective client with your mind focused on the discouragement from your last rejection, you will appear insincere. Your mouth will tell them how much you can offer them, while your eyes and body language tell them you're not thinking about them at all.

My first goal is not to earn a person's business or their respect. It is to earn their trust, so that they will know that they're safe with me.

If you let enough no's pile up in your brain, you will meet people expecting rejection and that's what they will give you.

DAY TEN

*"You will either step forward into growth or you
will step back into safety."*
–Abraham Maslow

My granddaughter is 6 years old. When she struggles to string words together to read a sentence in a book, we're all so proud of her. My wife and I are on the phone bragging to anyone who will listen. If a few years go by, and she's still struggling to string words together, we won't be boasting about it anymore. We'll be concerned that something is very wrong.

There is no area of our life where we are not expected to grow. Where there is no growth, there is death, in work, in relationships, and in individuals. Things were created to grow. Growth is actually the only visible sign of success.

Successful businesses grow in revenue or personnel. Successful students grow in knowledge and achievement. Successful marriages grow closer. Successful crops grow taller and stronger.

Potential has a shelf life. Possibility that isn't converted into progress through learning, experience, and maturity, will become the spoil of wasted opportunity.

Compare the life you live today with the one you lived just ten years ago. Has it changed? Do you eat meat in some areas where you once were only able to handle milk? Are you stronger? Can you handle bigger storms? Are you smarter, wiser, kinder?

Are you growing?

DAY ELEVEN

*"If a man love the labor of his trade, apart from any suggestion of
success or fame, the gods have called him."*
–Robert Louis Stevenson

I'm not happy on the job because I post big numbers. I believe I post big numbers because I am happy on the job.

We have to do more than just claim our right to the fruits of our labor. We've got to rejoice in the labor and see it as a gift.

How many of us really think of rejoicing as a responsibility and work as a gift? Usually we see it in the reverse. We're obligated to work, and if we happen to enjoy it, then that's just an added bonus.

Now, there's nothing wrong with that point of view... if you're not planning to do anything remarkable.

If your life's desire is to

leave every envelope un-pushed, every obstacle stand-ing, every mountain un-climbed, then simply do-ing your job without joy and without gratitude would be fine. You could spend every day succeeding at just work-ing, instead of working at succeeding.

But did you really get in-to this business to do just enough to get by? Is it your earnest desire simply to be-come good at being average?

If you're serious about what you do, then "good enough" is never going to be good enough for you. Ex-traordinary achievements await only those who are will-ing to take extraordinary paths to get to them.

Extraordinary paths re-quire you to see the unseen, live beyond mortal expecta-tion, and find joy in the plac-es that few have the courage to venture into because you know that the reward will be worth the sacrifice.

DAY TWELVE

*"Action springs not from thought, but from a
readiness for responsibility."*
–Dietrich Bonhoeffer

Development is as important as drive in our line of work. **Patience** is the ability to stand under any circumstance, in any situation, until what you're ready for is ready for you. Nothing planted springs up overnight. It has to be watered, allowed to dig roots into the ground to stabilize it and make it capable of delivering nutrients to throughout the plant.

If plants grow, but the soil or the environment isn't ready to accommodate that growth, it will eventually die. Likewise, if your volume of business increases, and you're not prepared for it, the business will suffer. Lots of companies fail not because they didn't grow, but because they weren't ready to grow.

The same thing happens to us on an individual level. Don't strive to make millions if you plan to treat it the same way you treated hundreds. If you're serving 20 small clients well, but you don't want to do the homework to learn how to handle more sophisticated clients, don't go after them.

No road to success is without its seasons of planting and waiting. Investing in a few workshops or seminars, when you could be pounding the pavement or making calls, can pay big dividends in the future.

To the world, patience can look like failure, a lack of diligence, or complacency. But, to the mind that is set on purpose, patience is faith mentally validating invisible things until it is time to receive them.

DAY THIRTEEN

"The reality of life is that your perceptions—right or wrong—influence everything else you do. When you get a proper perspective of your perceptions, you may be surprised how many other things fall into place."
–Roger Birkman

Circumstances do not define a life anymore than punctuation communicates the meaning of a sentence. I almost forgot that during a particularly difficult season.

The insurance industry as a whole was experiencing some hard times due to high interest rates. My family and I had just relocated, so I was trying to establish myself in a new, unfamiliar market.

In addition to that, I was battling some health issues, and, as if my plate weren't full enough already, I was going through the longest sales slump of my career. My confidence was crumbling fast, and I was being swallowed up in my despair.

I wanted to know why God

had allowed these devastating changes to occur in my life, so I went off by myself one day to a cave in La Jolla, California to have it out with Him.

I didn't realize it at the time, but I had begun to believe the biggest lie associated with change. I believed that I *was* what was happening to me.

When we focus on change, and not on who we are, we begin to allow change to define us. Abused children think they are worthless not because they are, but because of what is happening to them. If a brilliant, successful woman hits her head on the company glass ceiling long enough, she may begin to believe she's not as good as the male counterparts passing her by.

A sales slump is what happens to you. It may refine you, and force you to reach beyond your limits, but it does NOT define you.

We are what we repeatedly do, not what is repeatedly done to us.

DAY FOURTEEN

"Let me not pray to be sheltered from dangers, but to be fearless in facing them. Let me not beg for the stilling of my pain, but for the heart to conquer it."
–Rabindranath Tagore

Redefine failure. What I thought was a season of catastrophe turned out to be one of pruning, purging and preparation. Everything that drove me to that cave is being used to drive the men and women I would later mentor past their obstacles of fear and despair.

I celebrate every fire and flood in my career. I'm grateful for every dungeon and dark place. Fires burn up every bad habit and roll away every weight that could hinder our climb to the top.

Floods wash away anything that doesn't have a solid foundation. If you're not committed to your success, a flood will wash away

your resolve and your dedication.

The dungeons in my life
have taught me patience.
Slumps and unproductive
seasons are dungeons. Ev-
ery failure is a dungeon until we learn from it.

The blessing of dungeons
is not going into them, but
coming out. In coming out,
I have realized that dun-
geons are not my destiny.
My destiny—the reason for
which I was created—is to
succeed.

That means that all fail-
ure, and every dungeon, is
temporary.

DAY FIFTEEN

"Three keys to more abundant living: caring about others, daring for others, sharing with others."
—William Arthur Ward

I know a lot of people think that in order to be successful you can't allow your feelings to get in the way of what you're doing. I haven't found the way to do what we do without engaging my heart.

There is a reason most major corporations market themselves on a platform of dependability, care, and credibility. People don't entrust their futures to companies that don't care about them.

I am committed to people, not prospects. It's impossible to fail when you're committed to caring for people, because you will work for them until they have everything they need, not just until you make our quota for the day. I happily become teachable, change-able, and useable. In other words, I become *better*.

If our commitments shape our behavior, we can't help but succeed.

DAY SIXTEEN

"There is one quality that one must possess to win, and that is definiteness of purpose, the knowledge of what one wants, and a burning desire to possess it."
—Napoleon Hill

My toughest close happened long before I began my career in sales.

I love my wife Carol more than anything on this earth. I knew she was "the one" the day I met her, so I asked her to marry me on the spot. She turned me down flat.

But I kept asking. In fact, I asked her for 85 straight days. I'd go over to her house, cook dinner for her, propose, get turned down, go home, go to bed, and wake up the next day ready to do it all over again.

Now, another man might have given up after a few dozen rejections. But something outside of me, bigger than me, and stronger than me drove me to keep asking.

She said yes on the 86th proposal and 90 days after we met, we were married. My marriage, which is moving toward its 45th year, continues to inspire and encourage me.

Decision is that place between recognition and response, where we determine the value of what our spirit tells us.

If we decide that what our spiritual eyes see is the truth, we will make our mind up to act on it. If we decide that it isn't true, if we're too afraid of failure, or if we just don't care enough, we will decide to stand still or go in another direction.

Our action will always betray what we truly believe.

DAY SEVENTEEN

"Start by doing what's necessary; then do what's possible;
and suddenly you are doing the impossible."
—St. Francis of Assisi

You can't expect a generic set of principles or affirmations to catapult you to your destiny as if who you are and what you do today doesn't matter. If your dreams are big, you will not simply think them into being. You've got to live up to them.

All of us begin our lives in normal, ordinary ways. What separates an amazing life from a common one—or even a wasted or tragic one—is how we handle ordinary.

There's nothing wrong with wanting a wonderful life. You just have to be ready to deal with the "full" before you get to the "wonder."

Doing what needs to be done—the small, messy, menial things—is as important as doing those things that bring attention and admiration. We work our way up every mountain one pebble at a time.

Begin at the beginning with the life that is in your hands. It may not be glamorous, but it is yours. It's not supposed to be impressive at first. Still, appreciate it. Enjoy it. Learn in it and from it. Love the people who are there with you. Be grateful. Don't sit wishing you had a feast. Savor what's on your plate.

What have you been telling yourself lately about your life? How is your "inner script" shaping your performance, your joy, and your confidence? Is it centered on what you do have or what you don't?

Resist the urge to fashion a spectacular image of your life to satisfy your ego. Instead, choose to embrace it, as is, and value the beauty of it, even its smallness. Then you will begin to see the possibilities in it.

DAY EIGHTEEN

"To be of service means to be helpful. To pursue a successful career or to build a prosperous business in a service economy, you have to be helpful. The more helpful you are and the more people you are helpful to, the more successful and prosperous you are likely to be yourself."
–Joe Tye

We need to remember that people see what we do as a service, so we must have the heart of a servant if we want to do well in this business.

We're not doing that man or that woman a favor by listening to them and offering them our goods. They're doing us a favor by entertaining our presence. They are the ones giving out the privileges. We are receiving.

Servants are stewards, not owners. We have a storehouse of knowledge, information, products, and services. It is ours to guard and watch over until our "masters" ask for it.

A servant looks for opportunities to give what he

has to others. When was the last time you saw your work as something other than an obligation or a responsibility? Real service is providing people with something they value greatly, but cannot buy with money, and offering it with no strings attached.

If we don't make every effort to serve our customers, it won't harm them in the long run. They'll find what they need elsewhere. We are the ones who lose when we treat clients like beggars and not kings.

DAY NINETEEN

*"If you can, help others; if you cannot do that,
at least do not harm them."*
–Tenzin Gyatso, 14th Dalai Lama

Prospects become clients for new business. But clients have to become your friends for repeat and referral business. And the greatest gift happens when those friends see you as family.

Three months after I started at Prudential, I got a call from a couple who wanted life insurance. The wife was always looking ahead to their future, but the husband wasn't always convinced that insurance was necessary. He often threatened to cancel their insurance, so I made each of them the owner of the other's policy.

Many years later, the husband decided he wanted a divorce and he wanted his wife to release his policy to him. I advised her to stick to her guns, despite pressure from his family, and even their own children. Decisions made during difficult or traumatic transitions are seldom wise ones.

A short while later, he was diagnosed with terminal brain cancer. His policy covered his medical expenses, and when he eventually died, his family's grief was not compounded by the financial burden of his estate.

His children, who now have families of their own, asked me to handle them. I had become a fixture in that family, and because of the care I had given their parents, they couldn't imagine choosing anyone else.

You may not cultivate relationships with customers that last for years, but in the time that you do have with people, pay attention, and make your service count.

DAY TWENTY

"I tell you, the more I think, the more I feel that there is nothing more truly artistic than to love people."
–Vincent van Gogh

Imagine for a moment that you are not a person, but a well. How deep is your reserve of water? Now imagine that you are a palate of paints, available for someone to create a landscape of their future. How many colors are at their disposal?

Is your service one-dimensional or can you find creative ways to meet needs and instill confidence? Selling products and providing service is very different today than it was ten years ago, twenty years ago, and certainly thirty years ago. An internet search engine can give someone almost as much general information as you can. So what separates you from any other source of product or service? Nothing if you're not a student of trends or a forward-thinking servant.

Every client is different, but each one of them has an emotional map inside them that will lead you to a "need" or a "no, thank you." Where they direct you will depend on their perception of your knowledge, understanding, insight, and trustworthiness.

Listen to them with your *eyes*. Are they as certain about what they want as they say they are? What are they asking for that they cannot express?

When you discover your client's *actual* need versus the stated one, you have found their heart, their passions, dreams, fears and hopes. You'll know what they live for and what they would die for.

One caution however: People only let you see their hearts if they trust you to care. Don't go down that path unless you do.

DAY TWENTY-ONE

*"We could never learn to be brave and patient, if there were
only joy in the world."*
–Helen Keller

It's easy to rejoice over the more pleasant aspects of work. It's easy to be happy when people appreciate you. Work is fun when you're recognized and singled out for your achievements. But if we're going to be successful—if prosperity and wealth are to be ours—we have to become men and women who rejoice over the dry, unfruitful, ugly, tiresome, difficult things involved in what we do as well.

Our deserts have to be glad places for us. We have to learn to be full and satisfied in the wilderness. If it were not for dark places in our careers, we would never learn to reach past what has already been done.

True success is found on the other side of mountains, beyond today, further than our present understanding. The gift of work is found in its uncertainty, its hardness, its pressing, and its grind. Character and integrity are not forged in cool furnaces. Strength is not found in muscles that have never lifted anything heavy.

DAY TWENTY-TWO

"When you lose, you're more motivated. When you win, you fail to see your mistakes and probably no one can tell you anything."
—Venus Williams

E very shut door has a sign on it if we're willing to read it. The problem is we don't like to linger too long where we're not wanted. We think there is no value in dwelling on the negative, right? But, a hasty retreat might not be the best thing for us.

We must take it very personally when someone tells us "no." People seldom do it without a reason. Our job is to take that reason and make it work for us. If we see it as an opportunity to learn and an invitation to grow, rejection can sharpen us and make us better for the next encounter.

If you have the opportunity, sometimes it helps

to ask if there is anything you should do differently at your next appointment. That one person who is willing to offer you some honest criticism will benefit you more than a hundred books on the selling.

Suppose you did nothing wrong. When people reject what you have to offer, something or someone is at fault, but not necessarily you. If that's the case, wouldn't you like to know?

Don't be too quick to move on from a negative response. No may mean no, but it can mean a whole lot more.

DAY TWENTY-THREE

"If you pray for a Cadillac and God sends you a jackass, ride it."
—Anonymous

There is no power in regret. There is less power in wishing. Meet every day with the same question: What is in my hand? That's where your power is.

We are finite, mortal beings. We can only live in one place at a time, and that place is Now. Use the moments you have now. Use them up. Walk through the doors that are open. In fact, run through them.

Ride the bus until you get a car. Don't stay home. Eat beans if you can't afford steak. Don't starve. You don't wait for tomorrow. Tomorrow waits for you, so get moving!

Having success is one thing. Being able to hold

onto it is another thing entirely. The only way to have the life you want is to want the life you have, because the present always prepares you for what the future has prepared for you. Do the work you have, even if it's not the work you love. Prosper where you are, even if it pains you. Allow your life, as it is, to build, shape, and transform you. Use what's in your hand.

You may ask, "What if there is nothing in my hand?" There is always something. At any given moment, there are at least four things: **time, vision, attitude, and will.** Add to that gratitude for what was there, and hope for what will be, and you will have everything you need.

DAY TWENTY-FOUR

"Give me a stock clerk with a goal, and I'll give you a man
who will make history. Give me a man with no goals,
and I'll give you a stock clerk."
—J.C. Penney

Who you are is what you do, and what you do is who you are.

There are 24 hours in the day. Do you spend your waking ones facing forward, or looking behind? Are you a goal-setter who moves toward what you have to do, or do you find yourself reaching back for what you didn't get done as time flies past you?

Setting goals for some people feels like jail. All they can see is that their movement is limited, and their freedom is curtailed. That happens when we view goals the way soccer players do; as an end unto themselves.

Consider another perspective: One well-placed goal will give you more freedom to move than one hundred un-scheduled hours.

Ours is an opportunity-driven business. Time wasted almost always translates into lost revenue. The old saying is doubly true for us: Killing time is not murder, it's *suicide*.

Setting goals keeps us from being overwhelmed, because we plan for what's expected, and create space for the unexpected so that it doesn't catch us off guard.

If you have no goals—no apparent commitment to a path—it is difficult for others to take you seriously. Would you board a plane if the pilot said, "Hop in. We'll see where the wind takes us!"

Setting goals, and honoring them, says a lot about your priorities and by extension, your determination to succeed.

On your journey to the top, you can focus on the road or the map, but not both.

DAY TWENTY-FIVE

"If everything is under control, you're moving too slow."
–Mario Andretti

Tomorrow is yours. How soon you get to it, and how effectively you possess it will be determined by how willing you are to let go.

A little uncertainty and vulnerability are good. If you already have all the answers, you'll never ask any questions. You'll never grow. You won't push yourself beyond your knowing. A little chaos will keep you on your toes, keep you alert, and keep you humble.

You may have a very impressive career if you stay in control of all of it, but I promise you will NEVER be number one. You have to be a little worried that someone will catch you, or you won't run any faster.

Periodically put yourself on a learning curve. Find your limits and create a space for yourself just beyond them. Force yourself to respect greater wisdom, commit to greater sacrifice, perform with greater humility, and expect the unexpected.

Never be too self-centered to follow in someone's path. Never be too self-protective to contribute to someone else's success. Never be too self-conscious to tell the truth if you're struggling. And never be too self-reliant to ask for help.

Leap off a cliff once in awhile. Run in the dark. Concerning knowledge, make yourself a beggar from time to time. Cut a hole in your safety net.

I'm not afraid you'll die so much as I am afraid that you won't live.

DAY TWENTY-SIX

"A competitive world offers two possibilities. You can lose. Or, if you want to win, you can change."
—Unknown

You want to be the best at what you do? Always compete against yourself and then seize every opportunity to one-up your "opposition."

Take the first risk. If mistakes must be made, make them sooner and correct them quicker. Be the first to ask questions and find the answers. Sleep more soundly and wake up earlier. Make more calls, cover more territory, reach higher, dig deeper, and be more creative at problem solving.

The great thing about competing against yourself is you know your opponent. You know his strengths, vulnerabilities, and fears. You know what he's thinking all the time, and you know all his tricks.

You'll find him improving every day, but don't let that bother you. Once he gets familiar with your game, throw him a curve. Learn something new and show him a move he doesn't already know.

I warn you, he won't give up until you do. He knows you're better, so he'll play mind games with you to try to get you to quit or let him win. Make him pay for that.

Crush him. Every morning stare him down. Every single day, defeat him. Every evening, hand him his hat and tell him that you were better than he was...again. Then race him to bed, and get a good night's sleep, determined to wake up tomorrow and do it again.

DAY TWENTY-SEVEN

"You have a unique message to deliver, a unique song to sing, a unique act of love to bestow. This message, this song, and this act of love has been entrusted exclusively to the one and only you."
–John Powell

Every man and woman can leave a legacy of what I call "The Uncommon Life," that is a life that rises above mediocrity, reaches past average, and is never satisfied with mere sufficiency. That is the legacy we should all be seeking to understand, own and treasure.

An uncommon life is not lived within the bounds of cultural or social propriety. If that were true, Rosa Parks would have given up her seat on the bus, and Dr. Martin Luther King, Jr. would have remained a small town Baptist preacher. You don't ask permission to live an uncommon life. You grant permission for others to witness it.

It has been said that the great pleasure of life is doing

what people say you can't do. We all live with a secret desire to walk fearlessly into the place where we are not only welcome, but necessary. This is the place where our dreams prove to us that they were worth waiting for.

It goes without saying that the cost of living an uncommon life is high. It is never easy to challenge average expectations, especially if some of those expectations live in you. Do it anyway. You would not have chosen sales if there wasn't a bit of the rebel in you.

What we do is common. Success, believe it or not, is a common thing. The uncommon element in life is you. There's only one you. You transform the "everyday" into something special.

Dream your biggest dreams today. Unleash your imagination, confident that there is no place you can conceive of that your sweat and determination cannot purchase for you.

DAY TWENTY-EIGHT

"Friendship makes prosperity more brilliant, and lightens adversity by dividing and sharing it."
–Cicero

_____

_____

_____

_____

_____

_____

_____

_____

_____

_____

_____

_____

_____

_____

The greatest gift my 40-year career has given me is friendship. My clients are my friends first. When you have developed good, caring relationships with your clients, business naturally follows because friends trust you to put their needs first.

The closer my friends and I get, the more they count on me to handle their financial futures. They share their dreams with me because they know I care about making them come true. I also trust them with my dreams and allow them to help me make them happen.

As you look for ways to add to the lives of others,

you are added to. It seems illogical until you consider that you only harvest what you plant, and that what springs up is always greater than the seed. If you're planting consideration, generosity, and charity in the hearts of people, that's what they'll have for you.

When clients become friends, success is shared because toil and struggle is also shared. When clients become friends, they introduce you to the people who matter most to them, so you can help them as well.

DAY TWENTY-NINE

"He who is afraid of asking is ashamed of learning."
—Danish Proverb

Our credibility is our currency.

People don't care as much about what we know as they do about what we believe in. They aren't interested in what we have to offer them if we aren't heeding our own counsel.

Underlying every piece of advice we give them is the idea that they do not know everything and that **there is wisdom in asking for and receiving help.** How often do we take that advice to heart?

I'm not always the best planner. There are times when I can see my future in broad strokes, but I need someone I trust to pencil in the details. Some people have a gift for that. Has your understanding uncovered a need for someone to stand in the gap for you? If so, then your goals should include finding him or her.

It's tempting to stay on the path without too many attachments. It is humbling and uncomfortable to admit that we may need help. But consider that your asking for help may be another person's invitation to operate in their purpose. Would you withhold that from them?

The mistake we make is in thinking that soliciting help makes us weak or proves us to be incompetent in some way. The opposite is actually true. The willingness to seek help usually indicates emotional intelligence, security, courage, and an advanced level of honesty.

Excellence is almost never a solitary pursuit. If it were, I imagine this world would be in much better shape.

What shape are you in? If you need help, ask for it.

DAY THIRTY

*"If you think marriage is going to be perfect, you're
probably still at your reception."*
–Martha Bolton

There is a wonderful children's book by Dr. Seuss. It tells the story of a woe begotten creature who leaves his pitiful home to travel to a city which is fabled to have just one problem. His own life is so filled with misfortune and bad breaks. The thought of being just one problem away from a perfect life is irresistible.

He goes through floods, storms, darkness and all sorts of calamities to get to this place. When he arrives at the entrance to the city, he can hardly contain his excitement. It is as beautiful as he imagined it would be. There is even a key on the ground outside the gate and

31 Days of Wisdom

he rushes to it. He doesn't want to waste another minute getting to his new life.

He puts the key in the keyhole, but before he turns it, it is thrust back at him. It seems the one problem in the city is a tiny monster who lives in the keyhole of the gate. He refuses to let anyone use the key. The one problem is that no one can get inside the city. It is empty.

Life—or work—is never going to be problem free. Complaining about it won't change that. Quitting won't change that. Chasing such a life will only make you disillusioned or risk avoidant. What it won't make you is successful.

Problems are opportunities to stretch, and reinforce your convictions. Running from them leaves you weakened or unprepared for battles to come.

Don't look for problems where there are none, and

don't dwell in them if they are truly unsolvable. Some problems can only be dealt with by walking away. (They usually began as situations you should have walked away from before they became problems.)

Consider that all living things need sunshine *and* rain to grow. A life with no problems is usually not a life at all.

DAY THIRTY-ONE

"Thank God—every morning when you get up—that you have something to do which must be done, whether you like it or not. Being forced to work, and forced to do your best, will breed in you a hundred virtues which the idle will never know."
—Charles Kingsley

Once a year, I panic. Forty years in the business, it still happens, every January without fail. I wake up one morning overtaken by the realization that I am back at Square One, and I have to prove myself all over again.

It doesn't matter how good I was when we closed the books last December. It doesn't matter that I post big numbers every year. Come January, Top of the Table becomes a dream I have to chase again. All things are equal again, and I am standing in the mirror wondering, again, "Am I good enough? Can I do what it takes to finish on top or somewhere near it...

again?"

I once saw my wavering confidence as a weakness, a rookie's curse. After all, poise and self-assurance are the indispensable tools of our trade. Without them we are certain to end up in one of only two places: in a slump or out of the business...unless we choose a third option.

Fight. This is an opportunity to remind myself that I love what I do, that I am willing to do whatever it takes to remain good at it. I have discovered that this business doesn't just require my attention, it demands it.

Like a needy mistress this business insists, from time to time, that I declare my love for her and persuade her that my passion hasn't waned. So I give her what she wants.

I go to my office, pull out the files from the previous year, and I look at each piece of new business.

I remember each encounter, each call, and each conversation. I let my eyes travel over each note I jotted in the margin of an application. I recall how I felt that day, what it was like to hear "yes."

By the end of the morning, panic has been replaced by nervous excitement. I'm refreshed and in love again, anxious to write the first new business of the year.

What we do is not just a series of hellos and good-byes, meetings and phone calls, goals set and reached. To see it that way is to take all the joy out of it. Think of it rather as a dance, seasons, a river flowing, or measures in a song only you can sing. Enjoy it. Savor it. Live and love happily to the end of it.